M000039954

zen
questions

Project Editor: Nicola Birtwisle
Editor: Alison Moss
Designer: Elizabeth Ayer
Illustrator: André Sollier

Published by MQ Publications Limited
12 The Ivories, 6–8 Northampton Street, London N1 2HY
Tel: 020 7359 2244 / Fax: 020 7359 1616
email: mail@mqpublications.com

ISBN: 1 84072 293 2

Printed and bound in China

MQ 10 9 8 7 6 5 4 3 2 1

zen
questions

Robert Allen
illustrations: André Sollier

Why write a Zen book?

The author of a book on Zen cannot win. People who have some understanding will criticize because he has said too much, while newcomers will feel he has been deliberately obscure. Worse still, his publisher, who is used to paying for the number of words written, will have to be persuaded that the quality of a Zen book increases in inverse proportion to its length (my publisher has been a model of perspicacity in this respect!). Then, of course, there are the people who regard themselves as rational and hardheaded who will heatedly dismiss the whole thing as mystical nonsense.

Nevertheless, the task is worthwhile. The point of Zen is that it is not something that you can hoard for yourself. Like all good things, it is better shared. Nor is it "mystical" or beyond your reach. The problem is that it is too simple, like something that has been hidden by leaving it out in the open, which is the very last place anyone will look for it.

Can you really say anything new about Zen?

Although the stories and koans are all well known, each new Zen generation adds some flavor or understanding of its own. My own mission is to bring to an end the idea of Zen as a rare, exotic import from the East. Rather than resembling a delicate orchid that can be grown only under special conditions, I'd like Zen to be as common as the daisy and as useful as the potato. I'd love to see a generation of people grow up who feel that Zen is so much a part of their lives that they find it hard to conceive of the idea that it has ever had anything foreign about it at all.

Because of its very nature, Zen will never be a mass movement. It is too quirky for some people's taste. It is, however, the Zen way to want to share what you have. One possible way of doing this would be to demystify it to let people see that Zen could have a beneficial influence in their lives. Many people feel the need for a spiritual element in their life but can be put off by the idea of "religion." In many cases Zen could give them what they need.

Everyone knows the sound made by two hands, but what is the sound of one hand clapping?

Oddly, this koan is the first contact many Westerners have with Zen. Superficially it may not seem the best place to start but, then again, maybe it is. It is often the apparently unattainable nature of Zen that inspires people to delve deeper.

A koan is a question that cannot be answered by logical means. It has no answer. But you must answer it. In a Zen temple the students go regularly to their master and give their latest answer. Time and time again it will be refused. They will return to the meditation hall and try, yet again, to crack this hardest of nuts.

There is no single answer to any koan. There have been books of "answers" published but they are useless. The answer is individual to the student and, when it is grasped, the master will know.

And then?

He'll give the student another koan to crack.

OK, but what is the sound of one hand clapping?

A monk named Mamiya was given the "sound of one hand" koan by his teacher. He made no progress and the teacher scolded him, "You're too fond of food and easy living. And you're attached to that sound. It would be better for you to die. That would solve your problem!"

Next time Mamiya went to his teacher to answer the koan, he fell over and played dead.
"Hmmm," said the teacher, "you may be dead, but what about that sound?"

Mamiya opened one eye. "I haven't quite worked that bit out yet," he admitted.
"Dead men don't speak," said the teacher. "Get out!"

Poor Mamiya—he'd tried everything and was getting desperate. The more he thought about the sound, the further away he got from it. This is what makes Zen so difficult.

Usually, if you try hard enough, you will accomplish things. That's the way our parents raise us. It doesn't work with Zen. Not trying doesn't work either. Trying not to try is just a recipe for failure. A koan binds students tighter and tighter. They become completely confused and demoralized until, like Alexander the Great cutting the Gordian knot, they finally make one strong effort to break free.

What is Zen?[1]

Zen is

- Plaiting live eels in a bucket.
- Selling water by a river.
- Climbing the north face of Everest.
- Unintentional intention.

Your everyday life is very Zen.

Outside teaching; apart from
tradition.
Not founded on words and letters.
Pointing directly to the human mind.
Seeing into one's nature
and attaining
Buddhahood.

Traditional definition of Zen

What is Zen? [2]

Zen is simply the Japanese name for an experience that is common to all humanity and has been described in many cultures throughout the world and at all periods of history. The experience itself has no name, belongs to no particular culture or religion, and is extremely fickle in the way it manifests itself.

Sometimes people study all their lives, undergo rigorous training, and put up with many hardships without ever experiencing it. Other people, who had no desire to seek it, get struck as though by lightning.

Religions are, among other things, an attempt to provide a means of access to this experience. However, because those who have had the experience find it impossible to say anything very meaningful about it, and those who haven't had it miss the mark completely, the search comes to resemble a game of Blind Man's Bluff. The game is very much part of the experience.

Where did Zen come from?

It is said that Zen was founded when Buddha's followers asked him to preach a sermon. Instead of the usual wordy explanations he just held up a flower. One of the disciples, Maha Kashapa, grasping the point instantly, smiled.

In India it was known as dhyana. According to legend it was taken to China, where it was called ch'an by the master Bohdidharma (known in Japan as Daruma), and then at a later stage it was brought to Japan where the Chinese name was changed to something easier to pronounce.

In the 1950s a Japanese scholar, Professor D. T. Suzuki, brought Zen to the United States, where it gained a certain popularity among people eager to discover a new spiritual path.

Other Zen teachers, from as far afield as Korea and Vietnam as well as Japan, made their way to the United States. Among them was a middle-aged monk called Shunryu Suzuki (no relation). His enormous contribution to the spread of Zen was to teach that this was not some fascinating, but essentially unattainable, piece of Oriental mysticism, but a way of life that could be followed by anyone with the desire and determination to do so.

Is everything Zen?

When Zen masters talk it sometimes seems as though everything is Zen. Is my daily work Zen? Yes. Is going for a walk Zen? Of course. Is mending a flat tire Zen? Definitely.

That really doesn't help at all, does it?

Are there any things that aren't Zen? There are some things that are just trying too hard. There's a fashion for calling any kind of quirky inconsequential remark "very Zen." Sorry, that's not Zen. There's an idea that a certain sort of Japanese minimalism in design is Zen. This leads to books on Zen interiors, which show an empty room with two dead twigs in a vase. Sorry, that's not Zen. There's even an idea that anything Japanese must be vaguely Zen. The epitome of this is an advertisement I saw for Japanese rice crackers sold in "a sweet little Zen box." Good grief! When you stop trying, Zen will come of itself. But learning how not to try is the hard part.

There is no place in Buddhism for
using effort.
Just be ordinary and nothing special.
Relieve your bowels, pass water, put
on your clothes, and eat your food.
When you're tired, go and lie down.
Ignorant people will laugh at me,
but the wise
will understand...

Master Lin-chi

Does Zen teach belief in God?

Two elderly Baptist ladies knocked at my door to inquire whether I believed in God. I assured them that I did and they left satisfied. It was only after they'd gone that I realized I could, without contradicting myself, have just as well answered "No," or "Don't know," or even "Don't care." Zen is a way of liberation. It rejects all concepts, even that of "God." Once you name something, you limit it. Zen knows no limits. In fact, if you want Zen, be quick and throw it away!

Can members of other religious faiths practice Zen[1]?

Zen sees itself as only one of many paths to liberation. It does not, therefore, reject other people's beliefs. Zen itself, as opposed to Zen Buddhism, is a journey of exploration rather than the indoctrination of a set of beliefs, and anyone who wants to is welcome to make that journey. There is no reason why Christians, Jews, Muslims, or anyone else should not take part. However, other religions often have strict agendas in terms of what their followers are supposed to believe and not believe, and the free-flowing nature of Zen can sometimes be at odds with that.

Even so, there have been some interesting developments in recent years. Perhaps the most interesting has been the influx of young Jews into Buddhism in general and Zen in particular. The reasons for this are far too complex to discuss here, but the effect has been so marked that a Jewish friend once joked that Zen now has more Cohens than koans.

Can members of other religious faiths practice Zen?

❷

Gasan was a Zen teacher. One day one of his students asked if he had ever read the Bible. "No," said Gasan, "read it to me." The student read from St Matthew: "And why take ye thought for raiment? Consider the lilies of the field, how they grow. They toil not, neither do they spin, and yet I say unto you that even Solomon in all his glory was not arrayed like one of these . . .

take therefore no thought for tomorrow, for the morrow shall take thought for the things of itself."

"Whoever said that was an enlightened man," commented Gasan.

Do you have to be a **Buddhist** to practice Zen?

Zen is a journey of discovery with no map and no destination. You can make the journey if you want to, as long as you have no preconceived idea of where you want to go. Zen has a long association with Buddhism but the two are not identical. In any case, Buddhism is, by Western standards, an odd religion. It has beliefs and the usual quota of "dos" and "don'ts," but its followers also have a duty not to trust teachers (even Buddha) and to test everything for themselves. Buddha said, "Cease to do evil, start to do good," and, "Work out your own salvation with diligence." Zen says nothing.

What is zazen?

Imagine:

Have you ever learned a language? Zazen is the same but backward. When you learn a language you add knowledge little by little. Each day you gain a few words, a new phrase, maybe an irregular verb or two. In zazen each day you unlearn a little. You unlearn more and more until you reach **Don't Know**. This is not ignorance; this is real knowledge.

Imagine:

You look through the window and it is foggy outside. You go out and walk in the fog. The more you walk, the more the fog soaks your clothes. Eventually it soaks right through your clothes and reaches your skin. Zazen fog does not stop there; it then soaks through your skin and right to your heart.

How do you practice zazen?[1]

Basics

Sit comfortably on an upright chair. You can use a cushion to make yourself more comfortable but do not lean on the back of the chair. (Don't worry about trying to sit cross-legged unless you were born to it. It's painful, pointless, and obstructs your circulation.)

❶ Fold your hands in your lap.

Keep your eyes open. Everything that is going to happen will do so in the real world. Zen is not about self-hypnosis. Let your eyes rest on the floor a few feet in front of you.

❷ Shut your mouth lightly and breathe normally through the nose.

Count your breaths in sets of five. Each in-and-out counts as one complete breath. When you reach five, go back to one. Do this for about twenty minutes each day.

How do you practice zazen?

2

Finding the hara

Though unknown to Western thought, the hara is enormously important in Zen. The Chinese call it tan t'ien (the field of heaven). It is an area of your body just below the belly button. When practicing zazen you should try to draw the breath gently down into the hara. This may be physically impossible, but do it anyway. Don't worry about lungs and diaphragms—this isn't biology class. You'll find that with just a little practice you will start to feel strength in the hara. No, it's not your imagination. You really will find that the hara is a source of energy. The energy you generate in this way will be of great importance in your practice. Eventually you will start to feel the energy from the hara flow to other parts of the body.

How do you practice zazen?[3]

Bored, itching, staring at the carpet?

So you thought you could do it straightaway? Why? Could you swim or ride a bicycle the first time you tried? The first experiences of zazen tend to be uncomfortable. You may itch, get bored, or even doze off. As you look at the carpet you will see strange, sometimes disturbing, pictures starting to form.

In Western society, sitting doing nothing is considered lazy and irresponsible. Forget that! What you are doing will be beneficial not only to you but to others as well. First, when you sit down, do it as though you will never get up again. Don't think about the time you are "wasting." You will find that time starts to stretch like well-chewed gum. Soon five minutes will seem a pleasurable eternity. Beware of people who tell you, "My meditation is so deep that time flies by and an hour seems like only a few minutes." They've been asleep.

What is zazen like?

You know how if you drink alcohol the effect sneaks up on you slowly? That is very like zazen. You won't notice the world change in a dramatic way—in fact, everything will seem pretty much the same. Going back to the liquor analogy, you may recall that if you drink a little too much, at some point in the evening you may think to yourself, "Wow, I'm really drunk!" And that, too, is very much like zazen. You will get Zen moments, insights (which can last seconds, minutes, or hours) that will tell you that something different is happening to you.

Now comes the good part. If you drink too much all you get for your trouble is a sore head. The moments of clarity and insight you thought you had, the witty remarks you dimly remember making, all turn out to be a delusion. But with **zazen** that isn't so. The insights you experienced stay with you. Gradually they strengthen and deepen. Your character improves and people start to notice a difference in you. They probably won't know what the difference is, and sometimes they will only notice it at a subliminal level. But you will have changed for the better.

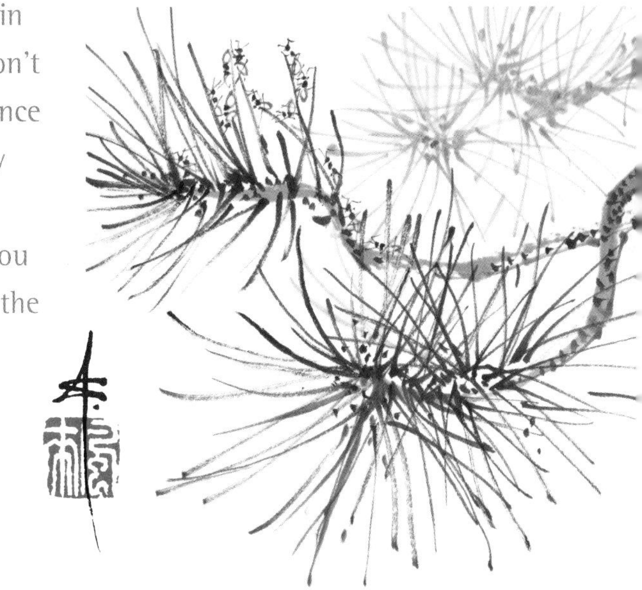

What are mind weeds?

When you try to sit in **zazen** you will find at first that you have a lot of distractions. Everything will bother you. Sounds coming from outside will break your concentration, worries will plague you, or you'll start to daydream. You may sometimes feel quite uncomfortable. Sometimes, more alarmingly, you'll experience optical illusions. The patterns in the carpet might turn into mysterious pictures, or you'll see odd lighting effects (there's an amazing one where you feel you are floating on a cloud of light).

Relax! Nothing untoward is happening. All these things are just mind weeds. Don't make the mistake of regarding them as some terrible nuisance that interferes with your practice. They are actually helping you get a feel for the mind and how it works. The trick is not to let them disturb you but just take them as they come. Once you learn to let the mind go its own way you'll find that everything settles, just like mud settling on the bottom of a pond, leaving the water calm and clear.

What is duality?

Good and evil, light and dark, heat and cold—these are all dualities. Traditional Chinese philosophy embraced these as yin and yang, each of which contains the seed of the other. Zen spurns them because they create artificial distinctions in people's minds. Of course, on a day-to-day basis these things exist, but for the student of Zen the task is to be able to transcend them.

Again, Mahamati, what is meant by nonduality? It means that light and shade, long and short, black and white, are relative terms, Mahamati, and not independent of each other; as Nirvana and Samsara are, all things are not-two. There is no Nirvana except where there is Samsara; there is no Samsara except where there is Nirvana; for the condition of existence is not of a mutually exclusive character. Therefore it is said that all things are nondual as are Nirvana and Samsara.

From the Lankavatara Sutra

The whole world recognizes the
beautiful as the beautiful
but this is only the ugly;

the whole world recognizes the
good as the good,
yet this is only the bad.

From the Tao Te Ching

Will you have a drink?

There were two Zen teachers quite unalike in temperament. The first, Unshan, stuck strictly to the Buddhist precepts, but the other, named Tanzan, was more laid back. One day Unshan paid a call on his friend only to find him drinking wine, which is strictly forbidden.

"Oh, hello," said Tanzan, "can I get you a drink?"

"I never drink," replied Unshan huffily.

"If you never drink you can't be human," said Tanzan.

"Then if you think I'm not human," inquired Unshan angrily, "what am I?"

"A Buddha, of course!"

Zen is not a matter of rules but of understanding. Unshan may keep the precepts strictly but he lacks warmth and humanity. How can you understand Zen if you are such a stickler? Tanzan may appear to be a backslider but he is wise enough to know what is important and what is not.

He calls Unshan a Buddha but he's being sarcastic. He implies that his friend is like a stone image. He has the outer appearance of holiness, but not the substance.

What are you carrying?

Two monks were traveling by foot in winter when they came upon a ford swollen by the rain. A pretty girl stood by the water, crying because she couldn't get across. One of the monks said, "Come on!" and scooping her up in his arms marched through the flood, put her down on the other side, and walked on. All day his companion fumed inside. Finally, when they stopped for the evening meal he burst out, "Why did you pick up that girl? You know monks aren't allowed to touch women. And she was pretty, as well!" To which his companion replied, "You're still carrying her, then?"

What you carry in your mind can be much heavier than what you carry in your arms. If you act from kindness and sincerity, your actions will always be right, even when others think them wrong. Above all, always act spontaneously from the purity of your original Self.

What is mu?

A pupil asked the master Joshu, "Does a dog have Buddha nature?" Joshu replied, "Mu!" meaning "No." It was a surprising answer because, according to Buddhist teaching, all sentient beings have Buddha nature. So mu became one of the most famous koans and is still frequently given to students as their first task.

If you want to work on mu you must put aside all intellectual considerations. Don't worry about the dog. This is not zoology. Don't worry about Buddha nature. This is not philosophy. Only think of mu. What could Joshu have meant? Just let mu fill your mind. You must think mu while you work, while you eat, even while you sleep. Above all you must breathe mu. You will not need a master to tell you when you have the right answer. Joshu will appear to tell you himself.

Will Zen make me crazy?

Some years ago a book was published claiming to give the low-down on sects and cults. It was written from a fundamentalist Christian perspective and had little sympathy with exotic beliefs. But Zen gave them a tough time. They couldn't find any greedy gurus grabbing their followers' money. They couldn't find people being indoctrinated and held against their will. In fact, they were hard-pressed to understand what Zen was all about. However, they had a solution. They said,

"Zen is a fine madness. But it is madness."

Is that true? Certainly Zen is not overburdened with a concern for common sense. Many of the things Zen teachers say are contradictory or even downright impossible to understand if you attempt to understand them using the usual methods. Also Zen people have a view of things that is quite different from that of the rest of humanity. So if you consider that makes them insane, maybe Zen is not for you. But it is a fine madness, all the same!

Oh, we're never gonna survive
unless we get a little crazy.

Seal

Is it important to be Japanese?

Zen is thought to have come from India via China and spread to other parts of Asia before it made a major transition to the United States and Europe. It does not "belong" to any one of those places more than another.

People who like to dress up in Japanese robes, give themselves Japanese titles, burn incense, and sit in the lotus position are fully entitled to do so. But that isn't Zen. After all, chess has an equally venerable Oriental pedigree, but would you dress up to play it? Change your name? Learn Sanskrit? Burn incense? Bang drums? Exactly. Chess has been so completely absorbed into our way of thinking that it no longer seems the least exotic and most players are only dimly aware of its origins. If that were to happen with Zen it would be a great step forward.

Zen is an exploration of reality. It is about your life in the place where you live, Here and Now. It is this immediacy that gives it its strength. It is not about a picturesque trip through a highly romanticized version of medieval Japan. Think about the way Zen masters used to give students a hard, unexpected slap. Nothing is more calculated to give you an immediate sense of the Here and Now.

Why does the Buddha have no baseball cap?

In former times Buddhism was one of the great proselytizing religions and was spread throughout Asia by adherents eager to find converts. Yet in each new country where it became established the Buddha was represented as looking like a member of the local population. So you see ascetic Indian Buddhas, slender Thai ones, fat Chinese Buddhas, and others who are clearly Japanese. This was partly because, with no mass media to inform them, the sculptors had little idea of what foreigners might look like and so they portrayed the Buddha as one of their own. Inadvertently they performed a valuable service. People were much less likely to think of Buddhism as a foreign religion.

The same thing happened in Christianity. How many images of Jesus make him look foreign, let alone Jewish? However, by the time Buddhism reached the West all this had changed. Now Buddhas look determinedly Oriental and the whole religion is seen as an exotic foreign import. An important truth has thus been lost. Maybe someday there will be a Buddha in a baseball cap and Levis who will put matters right.

Rinzai or Soto Zen?

There are two main schools of Zen, Rinzai and Soto. They differ not in their beliefs but in their methods.

A Rinzai master will rely heavily on koan training. He will confuse, bamboozle, and trip up the student at every turn. The student may become mentally and physically exhausted and, when this state of desperation has reached its height, the master will pull the rug from under his student one last time to produce the state of enlightenment known as satori. The training is potentially very dangerous and can be carried out only by a skilled master.

Soto training is a much gentler affair and relies on the student reaching maturity through many years of patient zazen. Much Western Zen stems from the teachings of Shunryu Suzuki, who was a Soto master. It has been said that whereas Soto students wait for the ripe fruit to fall from the tree, Rinzai students become impatient and give the tree a good shake.

Do I need a teacher?

The East is big on teachers. Whether you want to make a cup of tea or find enlightenment, you need a master to show you the Way. Buddha set out on his own to find enlightenment. He tried working with others but, in the end, concluded that he would have to go his own way. Maybe he had the right idea?

People will always enjoy joining clubs. The appeal of getting together with others who share your aims and opinions is clear. The trouble is that there are not many Zen teachers in the West. There are plenty of people who are eager to call themselves teachers, but their enthusiasm often seems based on a desire to be surrounded by devoted disciples. True teachers are rare.

Zen seems difficult at first and it is easy to believe that, unless you have a teacher, you will never understand. There is a Zen saying that goes, "Once you set foot on the path ten thousand Buddhas, bodhisattvas, and Patriarchs will spring up to help you." Just start your journey and you will see. It's true!

It is nonsense to insist that we cannot achieve enlightenment without learned and pious teachers. Because wisdom is innate, we can all enlighten ourselves.

Hui Neng

How long will it take for me to become enlightened?

There is an Indian story of a marvelous medicine that could cure all ills. However, it only worked if you didn't think of a monkey when you swallowed it.

If you think about enlightenment, you can never attain it. It is not a prize that you can win. As long as you see it as something separate from you to which you can aspire, then you are completely off track. Your own true nature is already enlightened. When you know that and stop struggling for a magical "something else," then you will be enlightened, but as long as you worry about wanting it, it will elude you.

You meet Buddha walking down the road. What do you do?

Kill him!

This is a traditional Zen question. It means that anything outside yourself that you call Buddha is not the **real** Buddha. When you understand that Buddha is the purity of your own nature, then you will not be bamboozled by someone wearing a monk's robe.

What is it?

I give you a small, round, red fruit. What is it? If you say, "It's a tomato," you're attached to name and form. If you say, "It's not a tomato," you're a fool.

So, what is it?

To take a bite would be a
good answer. To take a
bite, hand it back to me,
and ask, "What is it?"
would be even better.

What is "grandmotherly kindness"?

Zen masters make a point of giving their students confusing, irrational answers to their questions. They don't do it to be awkward, but because there is no way to "explain" Zen, any more than you can explain a joke. Either you get it or you don't. Even so, sometimes it is necessary to give the students something to cling to for a while, otherwise they will get discouraged and give up. Such explanations are called "grandmotherly kindness" because, although they are kindly meant, like a grandmother spoiling a child, they may do more harm than good.

Don’t know?
Good!

We are afraid of "don't know." It smacks of ignorance or, worse, indifference. In opinion polls we announce the "Yes" and "No" votes first, and the "Don't Knows" come as an afterthought. They are the dumb people who didn't have the good sense to vote.

What do we **really** know? In reality, very little. Most of what we know comes from other people, and often they got it from someone else. We think we know a lot. But all the big questions remain unanswered and unanswerable. There is really one huge Don't Know that is right in our faces but we choose to ignore it.

Socrates got it right when he said, "I know that I don't know." Although a Zen master would have asked, "Just who is this who doesn't know?" in Zen, "Don't Know Mind" is seen as very powerful. When struggling with your koan, if you can just hold on to Don't Know you will find an answer. Try it! Once you discover the power of your Don't Know Mind you are well on the way.

Who got it right?

A Zen master was giving a lecture on a hot summer evening. The room was stuffy so he ordered two young monks to roll up the long bamboo blind to let in some air. Each monk got hold of one end of the blind and they rolled it up together, being careful to stay in step with each other so that it would not go crooked. When they had finished the master turned to the other students and asked, "Who got it right?"

They performed an identical task yet one was right and the other wrong. How could that be so? Have you seen street artists who produce "perfect" copies of old masters? They seem to be clever and many people don't see the difference between the original and the copy. But however clever a copy might be, the genius of the original is missing. A Zen master can tell the difference between someone who understands and someone who is just going through the motions.

Is that so?

A young girl became pregnant but would not divulge the identity of the father. Finally, after much questioning, she named the Zen master Hakuin. Her parents went to accuse him and demand that he look after the child. "Is that so?" asked Hakuin and took the child from them. Of course, there was a huge scandal and Hakuin completely lost his good reputation, but he didn't care about that. For a year he looked after the child. He fed it, changed its diapers, played with it, and in all ways treated it just as though it was his own. Eventually the girl could stand her guilt no longer and admitted that someone else was the father. The parents, cringing with embarrassment, went to Hakuin, explained what had happened, and asked for the child back. "Is that so?" asked Hakuin, as he handed the child over.

Zen makes a point of nonattachment, which is quite different from detachment. To cling to things, people, reputation, possessions, and opinions is the way to suffering. You cannot grasp those things and, sooner or later, they will be ripped from you. People ask, "Why didn't Hakuin maintain his innocence?" Or, "Didn't he love the baby after he had looked after it all that time?" The point is that he did what he had to do. Compassion dictated that someone should look after the baby, so he did it without fuss. But he didn't get tangled up in "love," which is too often just a kind of possessiveness. So when it was time to hand the baby over, he was able to give it up without a moment's thought.

Aren't you lucky?

A poor farmer was returning from his fields when he found a wild horse. He managed to get a rope around its neck and lead it home.

"Aren't you lucky?" said his neighbors.

"Maybe," replied the farmer.

His son tried to ride the horse but he fell off and broke his leg.

"How unlucky!" cried the neighbors.

"Maybe," replied the farmer.

Soldiers came to the village and took all the young men to serve in the army. Of course, they didn't take the farmer's son because he had a broken leg.

"Aren't you lucky?" said the neighbors again.

"Maybe," said the farmer.

Our circumstances are what they are. To wish them otherwise is to fall into the trap of duality. If you think yourself lucky, then you are merely preparing the ground for being unlucky. If you feel you are happy now, then you must at some stage be unhappy. Why not take things as they come? **Eat your meal, then wash your plate.** That's Zen.

Where is the moon?

If you ask, "Where is the moon?" and someone points it out to you, what do you look at, the pointing finger or the moon? Zen is about actual experience. Nothing you say or write about Zen can ever be completely true because words are only symbols and Zen is about the things themselves. There used to be a feminist slogan, "A woman needs a man like a fish needs a bicycle." Likewise, Zen doesn't need anything superfluous. It points directly at reality. Even so, people are very good at paying attention to symbols and ignoring the reality that is symbolized. This is why Zen masters were inclined to shout at their students or hit them. Try symbolizing a smart clip round the ear!

Do ordinary people experience Zen?

A boy was racked with teenage angst. He worried about school, he worried about his parents, he worried about going to university, he worried about the state of the world, and he worried because he had no girlfriend and all his friends did. One day he worried himself to such a pitch that he simply ran out of the ability to worry any more. A beautiful calm descended upon him. He looked around the familiar living room of his parents' house and his gaze was arrested by a wastepaper basket made of plaited palm leaves. To his amazement this humble object, that would normally rate only the briefest glance, now seemed utterly transformed. It wasn't that the basket had changed physically. It wasn't glowing or burning, but it was infused with an inner glow like nothing he had ever seen before. It was only many years later that he realized this was his first step in Zen.

What do you need to practice Zen?[1]

Great faith

The faith of Zen is not faith in the tenets of Buddhism or in the words of Zen masters or in any particular teacher. What you must have is the faith that, for you, Zen is the right way. Once you take up Zen you will be embarking on a long journey that will last the rest of your life, and maybe longer. Although the journey will be exciting and exhilarating, it may also be very difficult. It will tax your mental resources to the full. If you are to make this journey, you must have complete faith that you are traveling in the right direction.

There is another thing you should know. Zen is not like learning an academic subject such as physics or accountancy. Plenty of people will tell you that Zen is by no means passive. Even if you do not have faith in Zen, it may have faith in you.

What do you need to practice Zen? 2

Great doubt

Zen is built not on believing but on doubting. You must be prepared to take nothing for granted, to doubt everything.

The emperor summoned Daruma and sought to impress him with a long list of good deeds he had done. In traditional Buddhist belief good deeds bring merit and a favorable rebirth.
"What is my merit?" concluded the sovereign.
"None at all," replied the sage in his grouchiest voice.
The emperor was not best pleased. "And who is he that addresses me?" he asked.
"No idea," answered Daruma, and left.

That doubt is one of the hardest concepts to get hold of. We are expected to know things, or at least pretend to know them. But without that great doubt you will never see Zen. If you want to understand the secrets of the koans, just raise the Don't Know Mind. You probably think that Don't Know is passive. It isn't. Once you understand Don't Know you will have the secret of great power. It's not a power like the president has, more like the power of a great ocean. And it all starts with Don't Know.

What do you need to practice Zen?

3

Great perseverance

It is said that Daruma spent nine years sitting in **zazen** facing a wall. Eventually his legs dropped off. In Japan they sell little Daruma dolls that commemorate the event. There are two types. One is a cylinder with slightly rounded sides. It sits resolutely on your desk as a paperweight while Daruma glares at you from under bushy eyebrows. The other has a round, weighted bottom. No matter how many times you knock him over he springs up again. The saying is, "Seven times down, eight times up." Both of these are reminders of the perseverance you will need for Zen. The road is very long and can be hard, unless you keep trudging on even when the going gets tough.

Is it
hot
in
there?

Zen masters are said to be able to predict when they will die. The nun Eshun, realizing that her time had come, asked some monks to build her funeral pyre and, when it was ready, climbed on top and had them set light to it. As the flames burned higher one of the monks called out:

"O holy nun, is it hot in there?"

"Only a fool like you would ask such a question," the nun called back, and then died.

Of course it was hot. Zen isn't some sort of cheap magic trick. On the other hand, once you understand the nature of reality, things are not quite as you thought. Why didn't Eshun scream with pain as she burned? Because she knew that hot is not the opposite of cold.

What are you doing?

A monk sat deep in **zazen**
when the master came by.
"What are you doing?"
asked the master.
"I'm practicing **zazen**
so I may gain
enlightenment,"
replied the
monk.
The master
picked

up a piece of tile and started to rub it with his sleeve. The monk became curious.

"What are you doing?" asked the monk.

"I'm making a mirror," replied the master.

"You can't make a mirror like that!"

"And you won't gain enlightenment sitting like that!"

The monk must have been bewildered. It's not easy sitting in zazen. It's certainly not the case, as some would maintain, of sitting on your backside doing nothing, or "navel-gazing." It's actually takes hard work and a technique of trying-without-trying that takes a long time to perfect. After all that trouble, you feel you have the right to a pat on the head. However, sitting in zazen is not the whole story. In fact, zazen is not just about sitting at all. Everything you do becomes zazen. It soaks into your consciousness and becomes your way of life. Until you understand that, sitting is just sitting.

Will practicing zazen lead to enlightenment?

Yes, but you should not practice with that end in mind because it lacks concentration and sincerity. You don't practice zazen to become a Buddha; you practice because you already are one. This is the expression of your true nature.

Amid all the uncertainties of Zen practice it is good to be able to hang on to something, anything. Of course, hanging on is not encouraged but, if you really need a straw to grasp at, then this is it. Keep practicing zazen and you will, one day, get there. Wherever that is.

Traveler, there is no path,
Paths are made by walking.

Antonio Machado

How do I find the path?

There is no set way of approaching Zen. This book and others may give you some idea but eventually you will have to follow your instincts. This may seem daunting but don't let it worry you. What you are trying to find is not something mysterious, but your original Mind. As a result, if you search with sincerity and diligence you will find it. In fact, eventually you will discover that it was never lost, you had it all the time.

Can
I
turn
back
?

Looking for Zen is not like looking for a lost coin. Once you start to look for Zen, it starts looking for you. People sometimes ask if it is possible to give up and go back to the life they lived before. The short answer is "No." I gave up on Zen twice, or thought I had. Each time, eventually, something drew me back to it. Nor had I gone "rusty" as you do when you leave other skills unused. It was very clear that, even though I had been unaware of it, my Zen had continued to develop in spite of my apparent indifference. I know others who have had the same experience. In fact, there are some well-documented cases in which the act of giving up was the very thing that precipitated the experience of satori.

There is a story of a monk who, after many years of trying, decided that he was never going to experience satori. He thought he might just as well make himself useful around the monastery, cleaning, cooking, and generally looking after the more talented monks. As soon as he made that decision enlightenment struck.

If you gaze for long into an abyss, the abyss gazes also into you.

Friedrich Nietzsche

薩摩道場

Is Zen explosive?

When I first read Zen stories I was confused by the way monks became enlightened as though struck by lightning just because the master made some apparently trivial remark. "Have a cup of tea!" the master would say, and the monk instantly became enlightened. Why?

Actually, it doesn't happen like that. You spend many years practicing zazen and your understanding gradually deepens. Then something may happen that causes the dam to break and lets the light flood in.

What I understand by "philosopher"

a terrible explosive in the presence of which everything is in danger.

Friedrich Nietzsche

What sort of Buddhist are you?

A Chinese carryout owner in Belfast shut up shop and was about to make his way home when he was seized by masked men and pushed up against a wall. "Are you a Catholic or a Protestant?" they demanded. "I'm a Buddhist!" cried the terrified man. "But are you a Catholic Buddhist or a Protestant Buddhist?" his attackers persisted.

This is an old joke about Northern Irish sectarianism but it does have meaning for Buddhists. If we take Tibetan Buddhism, with its bells and smells and love of ritual, to be the Catholic end of the spectrum, then maybe Zen, with its austerity and lack of fuss, is the equivalent of a Protestant sect. Brought up in the Church

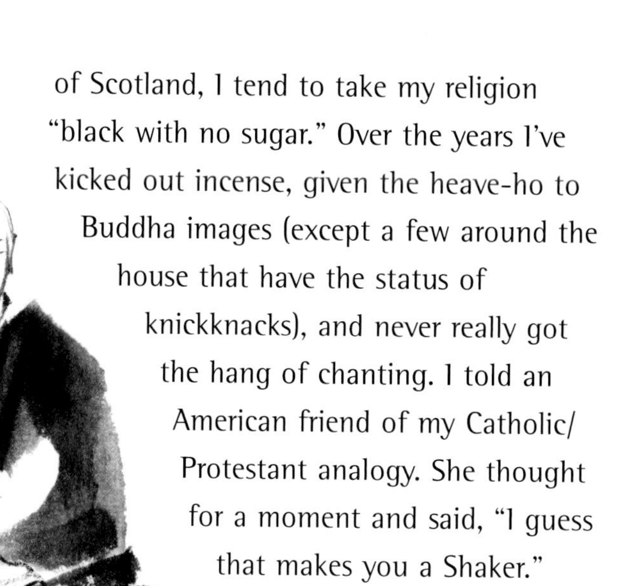

of Scotland, I tend to take my religion "black with no sugar." Over the years I've kicked out incense, given the heave-ho to Buddha images (except a few around the house that have the status of knickknacks), and never really got the hang of chanting. I told an American friend of my Catholic/ Protestant analogy. She thought for a moment and said, "I guess that makes you a Shaker." However, for Buddhists and Zen students this is all a matter of personal taste rather than dogma.

Is Zen violent?

Whenever a certain master called Gutei was asked a question about Zen, he answered by holding up one finger. His young servant thought it was a neat trick, so he started to imitate the master. One day he got caught. Gutei seized the boy and cut off his finger. As he ran away howling with pain the master called him. The boy turned around and held up one finger. The boy was enlightened.

People sometimes assume that such stories are exaggerated for dramatic effect.
I wouldn't count on it. In Zen terms, enlightenment in exchange for a finger would be a pretty good deal! But this is not really a story about mutilation, but about existence and nonexistence.

Is Zen violent? ❷

A master was approached by a young man keen to learn about Zen. The master would not as much as look at him. The young man decided to show his sincerity by sitting at the master's door to meditate. He sat there, day after day, for months. Still the master ignored him. Winter came and the snow fell, but still nothing moved the master's hard heart. Eventually the young man cut off his right arm and presented it to the master. Only then was he admitted as a pupil. The obvious point of the story is about the sincerity necessary to learn Zen. Would you really be willing to cut off your arm? But that is not the whole point. It also has to do with the disinclination of a true master to become a teacher.

Is Zen violent?

The difference between Zen and Zen Buddhism is most apparent when you look at the martial arts. The samurai warriors took Zen to their hearts because it was a Way that fit in with their style of life. It was vigorous, physical, and direct. It didn't concern itself with abstruse philosophical concepts and it prized spontaneity. The samurai were soldiers above all else and though some of them were also men of culture, nothing could be allowed to stand in the way of their preparedness to kill or be killed. This was not a theoretical possibility either. The samurai emblem was the cherry blossom, chosen because rather than withering on the bough it falls while still young and beautiful. No samurai expected to live a long life. These were rough, tough men who had little room in their lives for the Buddhist ideal of compassion.

In serving,
serve.
In fighting,
kill.

Jinzu

What is karma[1]?

You reap what you sow. Karma, a belief that is found in both Hinduism and Buddhism, is sometimes called the Law of Causation and is much misunderstood. The popular view is that bad actions have bad consequences and good actions have good consequences, which affect not only this life but are carried over from life to life. Whether your rebirth is favorable or unfavorable is governed by whether your karma is good or bad. This has led to a crass idea that poor, disadvantaged, or disabled people somehow “deserve” their misfortune as a punishment for sins committed in previous lives. This view is widely held in some Oriental countries because karma is actually not at all simple and blaming the underdog is, on the whole, more fun than pondering thorny moral issues. (This is not purely an Eastern position. A quick glance at many a Western tabloid newspaper will reveal a startlingly similar stance that does not even require a belief in rebirth.)

What is karma? [2]

Imagine you drop a hammer and it lands on your toe. It hurts, but is the pain a punishment for clumsiness? No, of course not, it is just a natural result of being clumsy. Next time, if you're wise, you'll be more careful with the hammer. So karma is just the natural result of our actions. It is quite easy to think of people who live so unwisely that they mess up their whole life. You don't need to be a "bad" person to do this; you just need to live without knowing what will make you truly happy. In Buddhism it is said that a bad man suffers as a bad man but a good man suffers as a good man. Both make their own type of karma. The enlightened one lives life in tune with the law of causation and makes no more ripples in the pond.

Is reality **really** real?

There is no room here for a philosophical debate and, in any case, in a Zen context philosophy is beside the point. What is more interesting is to ask **you** to consider whether you believe that the everyday world is as it appears. For most people the answer is an unqualified "Yes." What could be more obvious? In a way, of course, they are correct. As far as we can tell, people seem to experience approximately the same reality. People who are seeing something different (those suffering from mental illness or experiencing the effects of hallucinogenic drugs) seem distinctly odd. Also the reality people report is consistent—they wake up to the same world, year in, year out. Others say things such as, "I think there's a lot we don't know" or "I believe that someone looks after us." They accept daily reality but look to some other level of existence in which things are different.

For me, even as a child, reality never appeared to be the true story. It always seemed to be a theatrical performance. Although for most of the time the play was quite convincing, I could never quite get away from the thought that the scenery was painted cardboard and the heroine's dress was held together with pins. What has this got to do with Zen? It is just that, while Zen acknowledges that everyday reality is in a sense quite real, it simultaneously sees it as an illusion. If you can sometimes see the cracks in reality and if those cracks bother you, then you may be the sort of person who will find answers in Zen.

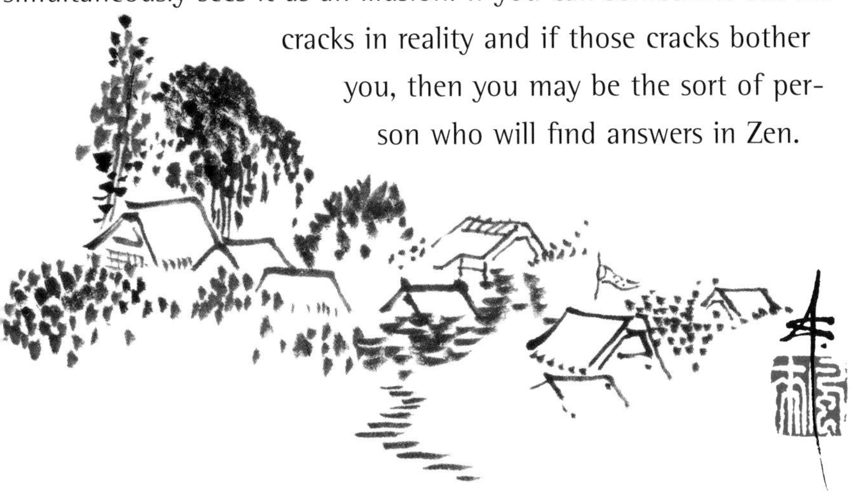

Do you have to be intelligent to practice Zen?

Hui Neng, who became the Sixth Patriarch of Zen, was illiterate and led a life of poverty and hard toil yet, according to the story, he became enlightened when he heard a man reciting one line from a Buddhist sutra. Zen is not an intellectual exercise. Indeed, all the critical faculties that are so essential to scholarly success are merely obstacles in the pursuit of Zen. Even so, because of its exotic trappings, its apparent quirkiness, and its reputation for being "difficult," Zen has attracted more than its share of interest from Western intellectuals. Go to the meetings of any Zen group and you will bump into more college graduates than you can shake a stick at, but you'd be lucky to come across a truck driver. Even in medieval Japan there was a strong interest in Zen from artists, poets, and samurai, but not usually from farmers or manual workers, so its reputation as some kind of "elite" sect is not at all new. Don't let any of this put you off. If you feel that you're a Zen person, then you probably are.

I'm a very busy person. Why should I make time for Zen?

They say that no one who lies dying ever wishes they'd spent more time at the office. Without getting too morbid, one day you will lie dying and what will your life have been about? Some people define themselves in terms of the job they do or the possessions they accumulate, but eventually you have to give it all up. Even people who define themselves by their devotion to their family or to some higher vocation, such as art or literature, all have to part with what they have become attached to. Zen is a way of finding out who you **really** are. Until you know the answer you cannot understand why you're living or what you're supposed to be doing here.

It is very easy
to let the rush and bustle of
life distract us from any deeper
thoughts. Many people welcome such
distractions because they consider any sort of
introspection as mere navel gazing. Others avoid
asking deeper questions because they have a suspicion that
they might not like the answers. If you do feel that there is more
to life and that you would like to know what that "more" might
be, then it is worth finding out if you are a Zen person at heart.

What is this life if,
full of care,
We have no time
to stand and stare?

W. H. Davies

Why are frogs good Zen students?

Zen has always been active in the arts. Those who examine paintings of the masters for a clue to what Zen actually is sometimes wonder why frogs pop up so frequently. Is it to do with a love of nature and compassion for living creatures, or is it something deeper?

Strangely, the frog is offered as a model of all that your zazen should be. The frog can sit still for hours, yet the moment an insect moves into range out flashes the frog's long tongue and the tasty morsel is gobbled up. No amount of sitting still will cause the frog to fall asleep, nor will its concentration waver.

What stages do you go through in **zazen?**

Imagine that **zazen** is a very long journey interrupted by irregular stops at places of interest. You will meet all kinds of stages in your journey. There will be times when you will feel marvelously relaxed, times when every night you sleep like a baby, even times when you feel an unusually high level of sexual arousal. Some of these stages do mark real progress in your development. For example, when you no longer see strange pictures leaping out of patterns in the carpet you will know that your **zazen** has deepened in an important way. The critical thought to hang on to is that none of these stages is significant in itself. It would be quite wrong to try to re-create a particular feeling just because you enjoyed it. It is quite possible that you could do it (I've never tried, so this is pure conjecture), but it would hinder your progress. The stage to be most wary of is the feeling of bliss. At some point you will become aware that all your worries and cares have dropped away. You feel you could sit like that forever, floating on a cloud. It's all very nice, and probably feels a lot like what you would expect a "holy" experience to feel, but it **isn't** Zen. First, when you stop your **zazen** the feeling will leave you. Second, although it is all very pleasant it is still dualistic. You feel good as opposed to feeling bad. So, although it's fun while it lasts, just treat it as another stage and travel on.

What has dancing got to do with it?

What do you do when you dance? Do you rush through the steps trying to get to the end as quickly as possible? Or do you relax and sway with the music, enjoying the movement and trying to savor the moment as long as you can? No contest.

Zazen is very like that. If you're overambitious and try to do too much you'll lose your enthusiasm for the practice and end up sitting uncomfortably praying for the end. Instead, you should choose a period of time that is within your capabilities and arrange some method of timekeeping that will warn you gently when this time is up (a loud alarm clock is definitely not recommended). Once you settle into your zazen, try to capture a timeless quality in what you are doing. Zazen can be a little like golf; some days you really think you have the hang of it and other times you will struggle. To go back to our dancing analogy for a moment, if you have ever tried the sort of dancing that has "proper" steps (as opposed to freestyle disco dancing), then you'll know the feeling that there is not enough time.

What if there
is nothing
on my mind?

One of Joshu's students was asked,

"What is on your mind?"

He answered,

"There is nothing on my mind."

Joshu said,

"Well, throw it out!"

To which the student replied,

"What if I can't throw it out?"

"Then carry it out."

The point of the story is that as long as the student has nothing on his mind he is still entertaining the concept of "nothing" and that's not good enough. Joshu tells him to carry it out, in other words to actualize the nothing in his life.

Can you practice Zen and still have a normal family life?

Although the majority of traditional stories involve monks and mendicants, there is a distinguished line of laymen who have played a vital part in the development of Zen. The sayings of Layman P'ang, for example, are still frequently anthologized and widely quoted. Also, there is no bar on Zen priests marrying and many of them do. In more recent times Shunryu Suzuki, who was one of the people most influential in bringing Zen to the United States, was a married man. Zen isn't about floating away on a fluffy pink cloud to never-never land where you sit all day thinking beautiful thoughts. It is about real, ordinary, everyday life. Living your life, with all its problems, difficulties, joys, and heartbreaks is wonderful Zen training. Some people feel it might be advantageous to go and sit on a mountain and spend much of their time in contemplative solitude. That might be pleasant, but if you can find Zen while standing waiting for a bus on a cold, wet Monday morning, then you're really making progress.

Is Zen safe?

Because Zen alters you fundamentally and permanently, this is a question you should ask before you start. The answer is not straightforward. Although not much will happen on the outside, your personality will gradually alter. The changes will be for the better (you'll become kinder, more tolerant, more patient, wiser), so this can be seen as an encouragement. People who start to investigate Zen soon come across passages that talk of "losing your ego" or "dying once so that you need never die again" or "the death of the self," and they begin to worry. Although all these descriptions have some truth in them, they are probably overdramatic. It's not so much that you lose yourself, it's more that you come to a realization that what you thought of as "you" was only illusory and that you are also everyone and everything else all at the same time. This is certainly quite dramatic enough, but it is probably less alarming than some of the descriptions you have read.

What has Michael Caine got to do with it?

(Not a lot of people know this.)

Michael Caine once gave an acting master class on TV. Until then I think most nonactors had rather assumed that he merely played himself and that there was no real acting skill involved in his performances. The program was a revelation. What was most impressive was the way in which he demonstrated how, by doing less "acting," he actually achieved more.

One of the young actors attending the class asked him how he would play a truly evil character. Caine replied that one way was to use a certain immobility of the facial muscles. With that his face stiffened barely perceptibly and at once became a mask of evil. The other actors were invited to try. They all produced self-consciously evil expressions that wouldn't have frightened a three-year-old. Not strictly Zen, of course, but nonetheless an excellent demonstration of the powerful effect of Not Doing.

Can Zen help with our present problems?

All this talk of enlightenment is fine, but you probably want to know whether Zen will do anything for you right now. The good news is that the regular practice of zazen has tangible benefits from the start, although the longer you practice the greater the benefits will be.

Stress

Zazen reduces stress. Initially this is just a pleasant feeling that you get from relaxed muscles but, as your practice continues, you will get a much deeper understanding of the mind and you will be able to control the effects of stress. You will also learn to avoid the kind of clumsy living that leads to stress.

Creativity

Because your practice puts you much more in touch with yourself you will find that you are able to draw more frequently and more deeply on your well of creativity. You will also find that, during zazen, the answers to problems that have been nagging at you will emerge.

Health

Your health will improve and you will become less susceptible to common illnesses. You may also find that you sleep better.

Our philosophy conquers our past and future problems. Our present problems conquer our philosophy.

François, Duc de La Rochefoucauld

I'm like a dog
sitting by a pot of stew.
It's too hot to eat
but the smell is so good
I can't bear to leave it.

Comment of a Zen student

To gain enlightenment
you must want it as much
as a man whose
head is held under water
wants air.

Zen saying

How much do you need **satori?**

The trouble with Zen is that everything works in the most unexpected way. The saying about how much you must want satori is true in its way, but it isn't the whole truth. If you strain after enlightenment, if you covet it in the same way that someone else might covet a Porsche, then you won't get it. You are simply not going about it the right way and, worse, you clearly misunderstand what it is that you want. On the other hand, like the dog and the stew, once you get a taste for Zen, although you may not be able to swallow it you won't be able to put it down either. Zen does not require desperate striving after a goal but it does take a certain dogged determination. If you take it up just as a hobby or amusement you will get nowhere. If you put in steady effort over a period of years you will be richly rewarded.

Is Zen funny?

The cook in a Zen monastery was delayed in preparing the meal. He hurried so much that, without noticing as he chopped the vegetables, he inadvertently grabbed a snake, chopped it up, and threw it into the pot. The resulting stew was much tastier than the usual vegetarian fare and the monks commented on how good it was until the moment when the abbot discovered the snake's head in his bowl. He summoned the cook. "What do you call this?" he enquired.

"Oh, thank you, Master!" said the cook as he grabbed the head and swallowed it. Humor is a very important part of Zen. It is not used in the way that a clergyman may tell a joke to show that he's really one of the congregation, it's used because humor, like Zen, cannot be explained without losing the point.

Is Zen relaxing?

In everyday life we distinguish between two states, activity and relaxation. This is a continuum with frenzied, stressed-out activity at one end and sleep or total exhaustion at the other. Most of us spend our waking hours at the active end of the scale and then, once we finish work, we slide into relaxation and then sleep. Some people become so attached to activity that they find the relaxed end of the scale hard to reach.

Zen is different. In Zen you find a state that is active, yet completely relaxed. But the relaxation of Zen does not subside into sleep. This "other place" is hard to find because you never suspected it was there. Eventually you will be able to sit in zazen with your mind completely relaxed but also totally alert.

Is Zen just quietism?

Quietism is exactly what it sounds like—the practice of finding tranquillity through a life of peaceful contemplation. Some people look at pictures of monks engaged in zazen and think that Zen is merely a way of giving up on life's struggle in order to live in peaceful seclusion. This is far from the truth. In Zen you find tranquillity in action, not by hiding from it.

The problem with quietism is that, as soon as someone or something breaks down your barriers, your much-loved quiet is lost. If you think of the samurai warriors and martial arts experts who were also exponents of Zen you will see the difference. At first you will find that it is hard to practice zazen except in peace and quiet, but when you become more adept you will be able to find Zen in a crowded shopping mall on a Saturday morning a week before Christmas!

What is "kwatsu"?

Zen stories often contain passages like: "Then the master let out a kwatsu and the monk was instantly enlightened." This kwatsu (romanized spellings vary) is said to be like the roar of a lion. It is used as a shock tactic by Zen teachers and sometimes by their pupils. It is not just any old shout, the person delivering the kwatsu has to put every ounce of effort into it. It is said that a master can tell how advanced a student is just by the quality of his lion's roar.

What is mindfulness?

If you read any Buddhist literature, not just Zen books, you'll soon see that "mindfulness" is a key concept. What it means is a little difficult to explain. The aim of mindfulness is to keep your mind focused on the Here and Now. To let the mind wander and engage in daydreaming, speculation, and flights of fancy is to remain trapped in delusion. Only by taming the mind can you hope to see clearly its true nature. However, this cannot be achieved by force. People routinely confuse mindfulness with concentration and this is a big mistake.

Let's take a pond as an analogy. If the water is stirred up, it will become contaminated with mud and debris. You cannot improve the situation by thrashing about; that will just make things worse. If, however, you let the water settle and become still, then the mud will settle to the bottom and the water will become clear. That is what you must learn to do in zazen. Do not concentrate on being mindful but let your mind settle gently of its own accord. Like everything else in Zen it is what you learn not to do that is important.

Chop wood,
carry water.

Zen saying

What is "before thinking"?

The American author J. D. Salinger wrote of a Zen monastery where the only rule was that if one monk shouted "Hi!" any other monk in his vicinity had to reply "Hi!" without pausing to think about it. There are plenty of similar stories including one in which a Zen sword master would creep up on his pupils at any moment of the day and attack them without warning, using a bamboo practice sword.

What has all this got to do with Zen? Your everyday mind, the one that calculates and theorizes and has opinions, is not your real mind. Your true Mind, which can be glimpsed in moments of spontaneity, is uncluttered by all the nonsense you usually carry around with you. The more advanced your zazen practice becomes, the more you will understand the true nature of Mind.

Why is there so much to remember?

Tenno, who, after many years of study, had passed his apprenticeship and become a Zen teacher, visited the master Nan-in. It was a wet day, so Tenno wore wooden clogs and carried an umbrella, which he left outside before going into the living room. Nan-in greeted him then immediately asked, "When you left your things outside did you put the clogs on the right or left of the umbrella?" Tenno hadn't the faintest idea and realized that he was not able to carry his Zen every minute. He asked to study with Nan-in and stayed with him for six years until he found true every-minute Zen.

For a Way that is supposed to be independent of words and teachings, Zen has generated a huge amount of literature that ranges in quality from very helpful to absolutely useless. It is not helped by the fact that neither Buddhism in general nor Zen in particular has anything that really approaches the idea of an accepted set of scriptures such as the Bible or the Koran. Instead there is a great rambling mass of material, to which everyone has added his opinion. Of course, there are sutras, which are accorded a high status, but these are only a tiny fraction of the material available for you to read. The result is that students get very confused. You may easily end up walking around worrying so much about whether you are being dualistic or mindful or sufficiently spontaneous that you forget to be any of these things! But take heart. Zazen is a very powerful practice and, despite anything else you think or do, if you keep up this practice regularly over a long period, it will work and you will get to the heart of Zen.

Empty your cup!

A cup of tea?

The Zen master Nan-in received a visit from a university professor and offered him tea. When the tea reached the top of the cup Nan-in just kept on pouring so that it spilled all over the table."Stop! Stop!" cried the professor. "It's too full!" "And you," said Nan-in, "are too full of your own opinions. How can you learn Zen like that? Empty your cup!"

People love their opinions dearly, so much so that they have been willing to suffer persecution, torture, and death for them. Even those of us who are less committed don't usually have much difficulty getting into an argument over politics, religion, education, music, or some other subject close to our heart. A modern Zen teacher wrote that you should be like a mirror. When red comes you are red, when yellow comes you are yellow. When people read this sort of thing they are usually affronted. Surely, they think, without my opinions I'd be a person of no intelligence or culture at all! Yet how often do our opinions turn out to be based on nothing? How often are they changed by the twists and turns of fate? Is it really worth fighting and dying for them? Opinions die hard. But as you get deeper into zazen they do start to die. First, you will find that you become less dogmatic, and then that you bother less and less with opinions at all.

Do not seek the truth.
Only cease to cherish opinions.

Zen saying

What does Zen say about sex?

A Zen monk became attracted to a beautiful nun at the same monastery. He slipped her a note asking for a secret meeting. The next time their teacher gave a talk to the students the young nun waited until the end then, on the pretext of asking a question, turned to her admirer in front of the whole assembly and said, "If you really love me, come and do something about it right now!"

Buddhism, like all the major religions, has sex rules. You can imagine them without any help from me. Zen has no rules, but insofar as it is connected with Buddhism and a monkish culture, its attitude toward sex has never been enthusiastic. On the other hand, there have been many famous laymen in the history of Zen as well as numerous married priests. Therefore sex is not actually banned.

The problem is that sex is one of the most powerful types of attachment we know. It is easy to get involved but very difficult to extricate yourself. This does not just apply to actual relationships but to other activities such as looking at pornography. Even a cursory glance at the newspapers brings to light stories of people who eventually got themselves into trouble but started out by looking at pornography they considered to be harmless.

If you want to practice Zen there is no need to live as a monk, but you might want to look closely at what you do to make sure you are not making a trap for yourself.

No loving-kindness?

A devout old lady regularly gave money to support a young monk in his pursuit of enlightenment. One day she decided to test his progress. She hired a beautiful young courtesan to go to the monk, embrace him passionately, and say that she had fallen hopelessly in love with him. Without a second thought the monk drove the girl away.

Whereupon the old lady descended on him in a rage, chased him from the little shelter he had built for himself, and burned it down. This may seem rather excessive, as the monk was only sticking to his vow of celibacy, but, as the old lady pointed out, while he needn't have given in to the girl, he should have showed compassion for her condition.

I love this story because it shows so well the human-heartedness of Zen. Too many "religious" people think that a self-righteous condemnation of other people's behavior serves to bolster their holy credentials. The young monk clearly thought he could prove his fortitude by strict observance of the Buddhist precepts. It never occurred to him that he owed a duty of compassion to the girl. He must have been truly surprised when the old lady burned down his hut!

Why can't the moon be stolen?

A Zen master lived by himself in a simple hut. One night as he sat gazing at the full moon a thief burst in and demanded money. "I don't have any money or possessions to give you," said the old man, "but you can have my clothes if you like." The thief was a little perplexed, but rather than leave empty-handed, he took the clothes and slunk away into the night. "Poor guy," said the monk to himself, "I wish I could have given him this beautiful moon."

This is a lovely story. It not only shows the Zen man's indifference to worldly possessions, but his desire to share what he has with others. What he **really** wanted to share, of course, was enlightenment (as represented by his view of the moon), but that is one thing that everyone has to find for themselves.

Dangerous? Yes, but delicious.

This story is attributed to Buddha.

A man was out walking when he came face to face with a tiger. In terror he started to run away only to find that he was racing toward a precipice. Having no alternative he climbed over the edge and, as luck would have it, caught hold of the root of a vine. Then he heard growling and, looking down, he saw another tiger below waiting for him to fall. His troubles were still not over. Two mice, one white and one black, started to gnaw through the vine from which he hung. Just at that moment he spotted a wild strawberry growing out of the side of the cliff. With one hand he grabbed it and put it in his mouth.

It was delicious!

For some reason a lot of people who have no background in Zen have come across this story. There is even a web site on which people offer their interpretations of it. Interestingly, there are many different ones. As in all good Zen stories the only understanding that matters is your own.

The story reminds me of a bamboo scroll painting I once owned. It was in the days when such objects were obtained only through friends or relatives who had actually been to the Far East. Mine showed a magnolia (it was chosen because the Chinese word for magnolia sounds a lot like my surname) that clung precariously to the lip of a precipice. Most of its roots dangled in the open air and played no part in anchoring the plant. The delicate beauty of the flowers was emphasized by the dire peril in which they existed. I was strongly influenced by the Zen spirit that the painting evoked.

Is Zen moral?

These are the rules that a famous Zen teacher made up for himself:

- First thing in the morning, before getting dressed, light incense and meditate.
- Go to bed at a regular hour.
- Eat regularly.
- Eat in moderation but never until you are satisfied.
- Receive a guest with the same attitude as you have when alone.
- When alone, behave as you would in front of a guest.
- Watch what you say and, whatever you say, stick to it.
- When an opportunity comes, don't let it pass by, but always think twice before acting. Never regret the past, but look to the future.
- Have the fearless attitude of a hero and the loving nature of a child.
- Upon going to bed, sleep as if you have entered upon your last sleep.
- Upon waking, leave your bed instantly as if casting off a pair of old shoes.

Few would doubt that, as rules go, these are excellent ones. The Buddhist, monastic streak that runs through Zen is full of good advice of this sort and, like all good advice, it is quite hard to follow. Even so, we should try to live as morally as we can. Nonetheless, Zen is not a school prize for good behavior. It is wild, unpredictable, and at times almost capricious. Moral behavior is not to be mocked but it won't, of itself, get you one inch closer to Zen.

There is a story of a Zen monk who, after many years of trying, could not find enlightenment. He went to his abbot and asked for permission to withdraw, which was granted. Having left the monastery, where he had lived in strict celibacy, he felt the need of a woman. He went to the red light district and found himself a prostitute. Just as they started to have sex, enlightenment struck.

What is merit?

A farmer's wife died and he was beside himself with grief. He paid a Buddhist monk to recite the Scriptures.

"Will my wife gain merit from your recitation?" asked the farmer.

"Yes," replied the monk, "and not only her but all sentient beings will benefit."

"That's no good," replied the farmer. "My wife isn't very strong and all those sentient beings will steal her share of the merit. Can't you recite Scriptures just for her?"

The monk explained that Buddhists believe in gaining merit for all beings and, eventually, the farmer was almost convinced. As an afterthought he said, "My neighbor is disagreeable and does everything to annoy me, so could you just leave him out of all those sentient beings?"

Merit is a Buddhist concept. It is found throughout Buddhism but is strongly emphasized in the Theravadin School. It involves heaping up spiritual points that will allow you to obtain a favorable rebirth. Merit can be generated by charitable contributions or, more questionably, by pious acts such as applying gold leaf to Buddha images and burning incense before them. In the case quoted above, just paying for a recitation of the Scriptures was sufficient to gain merit. The farmer learns a lesson about unselfishness. However, no real Zen students would spend any time pondering over what merit they had accumulated (the very fact that you thought you had some would indicate how spiritually bankrupt you were). Also, death and rebirth do not rate high on the Zen adept's agenda.

Shall I lead you on?

Ninakawa lay dying when the Zen master Ikkuyu paid him a call.

"Shall I lead you on?" asked Ikkuyu.

"I came here alone and I will go alone," replied Ninakawa. "I certainly don't need any help from you."

"All this coming and going is your problem," replied Ikkuyu. "Allow me to show you the path on which there is no coming or going."

Ninakawa was deeply enlightened and smiled as he died.

Ninakawa's sturdy self-sufficiency is typical of Zen. He had made great efforts and was clearly highly developed in his spiritual progress. However, he had not yet grasped the point that neither he nor anything else truly exists, and that there is nowhere for anything to come from or go to. Ikkuyu pointed to the truth.

Are heaven and hell real?

A samurai visited a Zen master for instruction, but he was clearly full of his own importance.

"Are heaven and hell real?" he asked.

"I see you're a soldier," replied the master, "but you look a very poor specimen to me."

"How dare you talk to a samurai like that!" the man shouted, and grabbed hold of the hilt of his sword to emphasize his point.

"Oh, you have a sword!" sneered the master. "It doesn't look very sharp. Maybe you use it for chopping wood."

With that the samurai completely lost control, and drew his sword.

"And there," commented the Zen master, "open the gates of hell."

The samurai, suddenly aware of what he was doing, put the sword away.

"There," continued the master, "are the gates of heaven."

Zen stories do mention heaven. However, these are not the places found in traditional Christian belief, they are mental states that are available to us right now (as the story graphically demonstrates). Zen has little or nothing to say about an afterlife but is very concerned about the state of one's mind. Life has many hells such as bereavement, addiction, hatred, and jealousy. Even love can be a hell. Anyone who doubts that these hells of the mind are less severe than the biblical sort has surely never experienced them. There are also heavens and, though these are never permanent, they do lead us in the right direction. In Zen you are not asked to examine the state of your conscience or weigh your good deeds against your sins (sin is not really a Buddhist concept). Instead you are encouraged to keep a very close eye on the state of your mind.

This very mind is Buddha?

A Zen master asked his pupil, "That rock over there, is it inside or outside your mind?"

The pupil replied, "We are taught that everything is an objectification of mind. So the rock must be inside my mind."

To which the master said,

"How heavy your head must be with such a rock in it!"

People have trouble with the ideas of body and mind. Anything that you are aware of must be in your mind. If it weren't you could not be aware of it. Therefore your body also only exists as a mind object. This is not some clever theory, it is obvious. If something is not in your mind then, for you, it cannot exist. If, for you, it does exist, then the only place it can be is in your mind.

Why did Kasan sweat?

Kasan, a noted Zen teacher, was commanded to conduct the funeral of a great lord. He was very nervous because he was not used to dealing with members of the aristocracy. Although the ceremony went well, throughout the service Kasan was tense and sweating. Afterward he told his pupils that, because he could not conduct himself calmly under such pressure, he was not yet worthy to be their teacher. He went back to studying Zen for some years and only resumed his teaching once he was fully enlightened.

This is not, as it may appear, a story about calmness under pressure. Kasan's fault was that, once away from the calm of the monastery, he was unable to hold on to his pure mind. He allowed sense perceptions to throw him off beat. A true Zen master would have considered even the mightiest lord as no more than another ripple in the stream and would have been unmoved.

Do you believe in ghosts?

A man's wife lay dying. She loved her husband very much and made him promise never to remarry. She told him that, should he break his promise, she would return to haunt him. For some time the husband remained faithful but, being quite a young man, he felt the need for a wife. He met a girl he liked and decided to remarry. Immediately the ghost of his former wife started to appear to him. She not only berated him for his unfaithfulness but embarrassed him by recounting in great detail exactly what he and his new wife had been up to. In desperation the man sought help from a Zen priest. The priest told the man to put some dried beans in his pocket. The next time the ghost appeared he was to take a handful of beans, without looking, and challenge the ghost to tell him how many beans he held. If she could do it, he would leave his new wife, but if not, the ghost would have to stop bothering him. The man followed this advice and, as soon as he issued the challenge, the ghost let out a scream of anger and fled.

The mind and its functions are of central importance in Zen. Although modern psychology and the Zen teachings about Mind would have little to say to each other, there is no doubt that Zen teachers have always been aware of how the mind works. This story is a good example of a man who, plagued by guilt, dreams up the ghost of his dead wife. Since the ghost is merely a projection of his own mind the only way to fool it is to ask it a question to which he himself does not know the answer.

Do you have to be poor to practice Zen?

The literature of Zen is full of patch-robed monks, mendicants, beggars living under bridges, and even a vinegar seller who is revealed to be a Zen master. You will also find frequent reminders that wealth, luxury, and easy living are not conducive to learning about Zen.

So does that mean we have to leave home and take to the streets? If so, there will be few takers. It is true that some hardy seekers after truth have made their way to Japanese monasteries where they have studied Zen, often under harsh conditions. Most of us are neither willing nor able to follow their example. Are we then barred from Zen altogether? I don't think so. I have tried throughout the book to draw a distinction between Zen Buddhism—monkish, rather ascetic, and sometimes straitlaced—and Zen itself, which is unpredictable, unfathomable, and ubiquitous. Rather like Ben Franklin flying his kite in a storm, the Zen lightning will strike if you make yourself open to it. Certainly, a penchant for easy living is a sort of attachment. On the other hand, isn't a penchant for poverty also an attachment (not to mention an example of dualistic thinking)? If you seek Zen sincerely, be sure that Zen will seek you wherever you are.

What is rebirth?

Buddhism proposes a belief in rebirth. There is really no "you," but the illusory thing that thinks it's you keeps getting reborn because it cannot break free from the cycle of birth and death. There are a few reasons why this might be the case. If you believe in karma then it is clear that your story cannot end simply because you die. It would be like the curtain coming down on a play at the end of the first act and never coming up again to help us reach the conclusion.

People who spend a lot of time practicing zazen are no longer impressed with the notion, "When you're dead your body and brain rot and that's the end of you." It soon becomes clear that this view of reality is not the whole truth. Buddhists and others notice that children, whose personalities are popularly thought to be the twin effects of nurture and nature, often show strong personality traits that seem to have come from neither source. Also, old people, even those whose cultural background contains no such belief, often feel convinced that they will get another "go."

As far as Zen is concerned rebirth is entirely beside the point. The object of Zen is to gain enlightenment in this life. Anything less won't do. You will therefore find very little reference to any sort of afterlife in Zen literature, but, because most Zen adepts are also Buddhists, there is an implicit acceptance of rebirth.

One world at a time.

Henry David Thoreau

Will I ever understand Zen?

If you mean "understand" in the sense that you might understand the rules of football or how to do quadratic equations, then the answer is "No." Eventually you will develop an intuitive understanding, but it will be more like the way you understand how to ride a bike. In other words, you can do it but, should someone ask you how you do it, you would be at a loss to explain.

What is more, you will be quite unable to pass your understanding on directly. If we stick to the bike-riding analogy, have you ever tried to teach someone how to ride? You run beside them, perhaps holding on to give them a little help with the balance, but nothing you say or do will bring about that magical moment when something clicks and they start to do it for themselves.

It is one of those Zen paradoxes that, the more firmly you hold on to Don't Know, the more you will understand.

Do I need to be a vegetarian?

Buddhists believe in the sanctity of life. Also, unlike many other religions, there is a belief that all creatures will eventually attain enlightenment. This means that vegetarianism is found in all schools of Buddhism, and Zen is no exception. On the other hand, some Buddhists do eat meat (sometimes having meatless days, or giving it up entirely when they reach retirement age).

In Japan there is the story of a shogun who decided to make amends for his violent past by strictly enforcing the Buddhist teachings on the sanctity of life. He forbade not only the eating of meat but also the killing of any living creature. Furthermore, should a person pass a dog on his travels, he was expected to bow and greet it with respect. Chaos ensued. Within weeks the country was ravaged by disease because nothing could be killed. The excess animals ate the crops and soon the population was reduced to near starvation. The story is told as a warning that, like all things taken to extremes, compassion can be dangerous.

What is the best time for zazen?

This is really a matter of personal taste. Let's assume that you are a busy person with a job and perhaps a family. You are unlikely to be able to manage more than one session of half an hour per day. Fine. That isn't a problem.

Mornings are very good. A session in the early morning before breakfast will put you in the right mood for the rest of the day. Unfortunately, if you are a beginner, you will find your mind is very lively at such an early hour and you might have trouble bringing it under control. Even so, I would suggest that if you are by nature an early riser, this is well worth a try. I always perform zazen in the evening. Being self-employed and working from home I don't have a long, tiring journey after work so I feel quite fresh at that time of day. People who come home tired might find the evening difficult.

The best way is to try different times and see when you are most awake and most able to deal with your thoughts. If you suffer from insomnia you could consider zazen in the small hours of the morning (preferably ending before 3.30 A.M., or you'll have trouble getting up when the alarm goes off). A period of zazen in the middle of the night banishes anxiety and promotes deep, relaxing, peaceful sleep. Try it and you'll never look at sleeping pills again!

What if I fall asleep?

It is said that Daruma got so annoyed with himself for falling asleep during meditation that he seized a knife and cut off his eyelids. When he cast them away they fell to the ground and took root, producing the world's first tea plant. Tea was frequently favored by Zen monks as a means of keeping awake.

In Zen monasteries the monks are prevented from nodding off by a senior monk who whacks sleepers energetically over the shoulders with a large, flat stick. You won't have this luxury at home (disguise your disappointment as best you can!). The place where Zen lives is right next door to sleep and this is a constant problem. Extreme measures won't help. If you're tired you need sleep and zazen will be impossible until you've had it. I find the best answer is simply to let yourself nod off for a few minutes during zazen and then, when you awake refreshed, carry on from where you left off. If you are really tired, give up and go and have a proper sleep.

Because sleep presents such a problem I always emphasize the need to meditate with your eyes open (rather than half-open, which is the traditional Zen method). It may seem strange at first but you will get used to it and you will find that, not only does it help you stay awake, it stops you from entering into trancelike states.

What is Beat Zen?

The Beats were a phenomenon of postwar America. The names you hear most often associated with the movement were those of

Jack Kerouac,

Allen Ginsberg,

and Lawrence Ferlinghetti,

although there are plenty of others. They were writers, poets, artists, and musicians who lived a rather dissolute life that involved traveling across America sampling all that life had to offer. They were widely condemned for their involvement with casual sex and illegal drugs. Some of them became interested in Buddhism and, particularly, in Zen. This interest was not welcomed by the rather uptight and resolutely middle-class groups who regarded Zen as their own territory. The Beats did little harm, except to themselves; they genuinely wanted to explore (even down dangerous paths), and this exploration is very much in the Zen tradition. Their writings attracted people to the study of Zen who might otherwise have missed out. Although they are not important figures in Zen history, they do not deserve the odium that is heaped on them.

Is Zen just a game for the quick-witted?

When a monk asked Ummon, "What is Buddha?" he answered, "Dry dung."

When a monk asked Baso, "What is Buddha?" he answered, "This mind is not Buddha."

For people with no background in Zen it often sounds like some sort of word game or weird lateral thinking puzzle. Zen masters not only don't give "straight" answers, they seldom give the same answer twice. But are the answers simply meaningless? No, that's not it either.

If you feel confused, that's fine. You are meant, at this stage, to feel confused. You have been trained from birth to think a certain way. You have been conditioned to believe that this is the only way to think and that all sane people do as you do. Zen seeks to break this stranglehold and introduce you to the possibility that you, and everybody else, have got it wrong. Upsetting the logic cart is part of this process.

Don't worry if you can't grasp what is going on. It is not an intellectual exercise. If you thought you could grasp it you would be doing it wrong. However, as you progress with your Zen training you will increasingly smile to yourself as you think,

"Oh, so that's what he meant!"

Here I
stand,
I can do
no other,
God
help me.
Amen.

Martin Luther

How did Martin Luther get in here?

My uncle, a clergyman of the fire-breathing Protestant persuasion, once gave me a commemorative medal with Martin Luther's prayer on one side and a picture of the great man on the other. At the age of nine I was unimpressed. I thought the prayer sounded pretty feeble. When I was older and had more sense, a lot of things fell into place. Luther realized that there is nothing you can do to get It. He even realized that it is quite pointless, in spite of everything that holy people and holy books tell you, to speculate on what It might actually be. If, however, you lay yourself open to the experience, then It might strike you like lightning. His prayer was not, as I had once imagined, about weakness and surrender, but about opening yourself to something you are quite unable to comprehend and being willing to let it take over you. People who hope to get It by faith or by good works are, however well intentioned, misguided. Eventually you have to let the lightning strike. Zen practice is a lot to do with making yourself available to that experience.

What about the starving children?

Whenever you talk about Zen someone will eventually say something like,

"Yes, that's all very well, but what about the starving children in Sudan?"

The group they mention will change according to the latest world catastrophe to appear on TV but the implication is always that Zen may be very fine for comfortable middle-class people, but it's not much use to those in starving, war-torn countries. This is completely true, but then Zen presents itself, not as a universal panacea like Christianity, but as a way of liberation for those suited to it. Many of the things we value (democracy, electricity, art, ice cream, newspapers, and television, to name just a few) are not available to huge numbers of the world's people, but this does not mean that we must abandon such things as if they were of no value. Zen encourages compassion. It is one of the very best ways of getting to work on yourself and refining your character (which is not the same as saying that all Zen followers are instant saints!). However, if you think that Zen will help to save the world in the Western sense, then you will be disappointed.

Can I join a group?

In spite of my distaste for groups (I belong to the Grumpy Old Man School of Zen), some people actually enjoy the fellowship (or sistership) of working with others. Why not? If you live in the United States nothing could be simpler than finding a Zen group. Nowadays they exist not only in obvious places such as Los Angeles but even in cities such as Houston, Texas, which you might think an unlikely site for a thriving Zen community.

Most of the groups seem to be represented on the Internet (just type "Zen" into a search engine and you will get more information than you know what to do with). In my experience American groups will make foreigners welcome and, as far as is possible at a distance, will allow you to join in with their activities. At the very least there is usually someone who will answer your questions and offer advice on your progress.

If you live outside the United States you will find it less easy. There are European groups and, once again, the Internet is the easiest way to find them. However, they are not plentiful; the Zen tradition has not really caught on to any great extent in Europe. However, Buddhism has the advantage of not being sectarian and, if you are interested, you will find organizations such as the Buddhist Centre in Cambridge, England, that welcomes Buddhists of all flavors (although its emphasis is mainly Theravadin).

Are there any things I should be wary of when practicing zazen?

Zazen is beneficial in almost any way you can think of. People do, however, tend to be surprised at just how physical the results can be. The energy that you generate flows around the body in a way that, until you are used to it, can be rather uncomfortable. The nearest feeling I can liken it to is the rush of adrenalin-rich blood caused by a session of hard exercise. If you thought that Zen was going to be somehow "spiritual" you are in for a big surprise. The whole experience takes place on what most people would regard as the physical level and, although it will eventually become quite familiar and comforting, it may make you feel a little odd until you are used to it. The one rather unpleasant thing that happens (not, in my experience, very often) is a slight headache like the one you get from inhaling very cold air. This can be a nuisance and make you rather tetchy, but it doesn't happen often and it soon goes away.

Can anyone practice Zen?

The short answer is "no."

Zen suits certain people. As far as I can tell, they are not a certain **type** of person (I have never noticed any other common characteristics), but there are individuals who are definitely Zen people. If you are one, you will probably know it. I remember wanting Zen even before I had any clear idea of what it was. I read a book on Buddhism, and when I reached the Zen chapter I immediately thought, "Yes!" Another thing that Zen people often experience is the feeling that Zen is not merely a passive "subject" like French or Trigonometry, but that it is in some way active. In other words, Zen may choose you whether you like it or not. Those of a rational disposition will, of course, dismiss any such mystical notion. Unless they are chosen . . .

If you feel that Zen might be for you, the only way to find out is to try. Allow for the fact that zazen won't be easy at first and has to be learned. A couple of months of effort should tell you whether Zen is your Way or whether you should look for another.

Is everything I do zazen?

A young American mother went on to a Zen e-mail list I subscribe to and expressed her frustration that, because of her parenting duties, she never had time to practice **zazen** any more. Her teacher pointed out that looking after a baby was **zazen** and there would be plenty of time for sitting on a cushion with her legs crossed when the child was older.

Yes, absolutely everything you do is zazen.

Or at least it will be when you know what this rather irritating statement actually means. This always sounds like one of those pious sentiments, "All men are brothers," which, although true in a theoretical kind of way, is not much help to anyone. At some point someone who thinks he's clever usually drags up some mundane act (for some Freudian reason it usually involves excretion) and says, "Is that zazen?" Yes, of course it is! As your practice ripens it becomes less and less distinguishable from your "normal" life. Zazen is, as I never tire of saying, not a matter of sitting in a trance thinking beautiful thoughts. It is all about being Here and Now and expressing your true Self in the simplest and most direct way possible. The reason it is so difficult is exactly because it is just so blindingly simple.

What is samadhi?

Strictly speaking, samadhi refers to the final step on the road to enlightenment. The word is also used rather loosely to mean an advanced state of meditation. Unfortunately, people tend to use words like "profound" in connection with samadhi. This gives a false impression that it involves some deep trance. During a question-and-answer session someone once asked a Zen teacher whether an enlightened person still needed to perform zazen. The answer was yes, but he added that someone who was enlightened would only need to take a couple of breaths to enter a "deep samadhi." Although this was true enough, it gave the unfortunate impression that those who have experienced enlightenment are permanently "away with the fairies."

My family tell me things that have happened that they are convinced I am ignorant of because "you were doing your meditation when it happened." In vain I tell them that not only was I not on another planet or higher astral plane but that I could hear quite plainly and in minute detail everything that was going on in the house, including all the things (such as the doves cooing on the roof) that they didn't hear. They take no notice. It seems obvious to them that anyone who is meditating is no longer of this earth.

What is samsara?

Samsara is the name Buddhists give to the world of birth and death, the "normal" world that you inhabit every day. That sounds simple enough, until you are told that the everyday world is also the world of enlightenment. How can that be? Truly there is only one world. At no stage will there be a blinding flash after which you will find yourself transported to paradise. Zen isn't like that. It is much more like one of those trick pictures that looks like an old lady until, suddenly, you change your point of view and see the picture of a young girl. The difference is that, whereas both trick pictures are equally valid, in Zen only one of the views is the real one.

How often should I meditate?

Meditation is important to Zen but it is not, by any means, the whole thing. As I have said elsewhere, there comes a point where anything you do is zazen. The formal sitting is good training and you will find it deeply satisfying, but you must not let it reach the point where you are enslaved by it. Imagine you had a box of tools but always chose to use the hammer. What sort of carpenter would you be?

I usually meditate each evening, but I try not to get so attached to my practice that if for some reason I can't do it, I start to feel upset. That sort of attachment is a hindrance to your understanding. Zen should suffuse your whole life. More than that, Zen *is* your whole life.

If you read Zen literature you will find tales of people undertaking heroic meditation sessions. One of the most famous is Daruma, who is said to have faced the wall for nine years. While you will have no trouble in taking this with a pinch of salt, you might be more overawed by tales of Zen students who meditate for ten hours a day. Although this is true, it is not a daily practice. In Zen centers it is usual to have regular concentrated periods of meditation that last up to a week. This grand effort serves to push people over the brink into satori. You might find this more than you are ready to undertake. Never mind. Short periods of half an hour or so are enough to help you make real progress.

Meditation is not
a means to an end.
It is both the means
and the end.

Krishnamurti

How do you know that satori really exists?

This is a good question and one people are entitled to ask. In all conscience I cannot tell you that I have ever met someone who has experienced satori. There are numerous stories, both ancient and modern, of people who have had this experience. Many of these stories are quite believable (a few seem rather suspect) but finding someone who is willing to claim a satori experience is not easy. The matter is not helped when even a respected teacher such as Shunryu Suzuki proclaimed that he never had satori. As your Zen training progresses you begin to suspect that the problem is not that you are being fooled by a bunch of charlatans, but that your understanding of Zen and satori were just not sufficiently profound.

To experience **satori** you need to build up a considerable head of steam. You must confront Don't Know with all your might and, once you get to the point where you are completely paralysed by it, the dam will break. Most people outside Japan practice in a much gentler way. They let their understanding ripen slowly over a period of many years and therefore probably never have a sudden enlightenment experience. That does not mean that they do not become enlightened.

Are you enlightened?

Talk about Zen for long enough and someone, usually wearing a jolly but faintly mocking grin, will say, "What about you, then, are *you* enlightened?" This is a troublesome question. If you admit to not being enlightened, people have every right to question your right to offer advice about Zen at all. If you were to claim enlightenment, then your problems would really begin. People would expect you to walk on water and then feed the five thousand as an encore. One could always say something mysterious and Zenlike ("The sky is blue, the clouds are white," sounds suitably mystical) to avoid the issue, but I'm sure that's cheating.

Imagine you were an artist and someone asked you, "Are you a great artist?" What would you reply? Enlightenment is a bit like that. What I say is that I have studied Zen for twenty-five years. Anyone is welcome to the fruits of my study for what they are worth. But they will have to decide for themselves if I'm worth listening to, because that is not really a decision for me to make.

Can Zen masters perform miracles?

I could be wrong, but I think that Zen is the only spiritual discipline that accepts that adepts can perform miracles but regards that ability with the very deepest suspicion. I have never heard of any Zen master gaining points for performing miracles. There are a couple of stories that make the point.

One is of a master who saw one of his senior students crossing a river by walking on the water. "Come here!" he bellowed. He led the student a mile downriver to a ferry and ushered him on board. "This," he said sternly, "is how you cross a river."

In another story two monks were traveling together when they reached a river swollen by rain. One of them took off his hat, cast it into the flood, then stood on it to float across. "Ha!" spat his disgusted companion. "If I'd known he was that sort of fellow I'd have broken both his legs!"

Is mind really pure?

The Korean master Seung Sahn said, "Clear mind is like the full moon in the sky. Sometimes clouds come and cover it, but the moon is always behind them. Clouds go away and the moon shines brightly. So don't worry about clear mind, it is always there."

The Zen view of mind is so different from the one most of us grew up with that it comes as a huge shock. If you were brought up in one of the big three monotheistic religions you will be familiar with the idea that, at bottom, you are a sinner and that unless you are redeemed in some way (depending on which religion you belong to), there is no hope for you. The Buddhist view is that our original mind is pure. In fact, since Mind is all there is, nothing anyone can do could possibly make it impure.

People may, of course, be stupid, ignorant, cruel, lustful, greedy, or hateful, but they are not evil. It is rather as if you had been rolling in straw and got your clothes filthy. There is no doubt about how dirty you look but the dirt is not you, it is something you have acquired and is stuck on to the real you which, underneath, is still perfectly clean.

This idea of an originally pure mind is fundamental to Zen. It underlies all the talk of spontaneity and doing things "before thinking." It puts Zen at odds not only with some of the major religions, but with psychological theory. Freud and others may not have been convinced of original sin, but they were pretty sure that the mind was a murky and dangerous place inhabited by monsters (monsters which they, at a price, were uniquely qualified to slay). The idea that there is nothing wrong with you has come as a great relief to many people who were tired of carrying this burden of guilt and blame.

What is nirvana?

Nirvana is sometimes thought of, even by Buddhists who should know better, as the Buddhist version of heaven. Others, a little more sophisticated in their views, see it as a supremely elevated mental state. Clues given by patriarchs of the past are confusing. One saying goes, "To those who say that Nirvana is to cease,

tell them they err.

To those who say that Nirvana is to exist,

tell them they lie."

As you continue your Zen training you increasingly feel that you are not just in the universe, but that you are it and it is you. Think of a block of ice floating in the sea. Is the ice different from the sea? In form it may be but fundamentally they are the same. When the ice melts is it lost? Of course not. The ice is the sea and the sea is the ice. This is fine as an intellectual concept but it is when you feel this in the marrow of your bones that you will know what Nirvana is.

Why is Zen so full of contradictions?

Zen is mind only.
Zen is no mind.

The Buddha is three pounds of flax.
You are the Buddha.

The contradictory nature of Zen is legendary. Some people find it totally infuriating. They feel that when the meanings of words are undermined in this way the whole basis of our world is being undermined–which is precisely the point. Words are symbols; they are not the real thing. We all know that, of course, but because we use those symbols all the time we inevitably get caught up in them. Zen unravels the mental tangle and forces students to look at what is actually right in front of them. When this starts to happen it is an odd experience. You assume that you have been looking at the world all along only to discover that, at best, you have been seeing it through a set of dirty old lace curtains that obscured your view.

Is this all a lot of fuss about nothing?

When Chinese Taoism collided with Buddhism from India the result was not religious intolerance but a new flowering of understanding. One thing that Taoism and Zen have in common is a great respect for nonexistence. They do not consider an absence of phenomena to be a mere nothingness. On the contrary, nonexistence can be very powerful.

Japanese friends once took me to view a painting exhibition. There was a vast painting of the confluence of two rivers, which particularly impressed me. From close up it looked scarcely more than blank paper with a few dabs of watery ink. However, viewed from a suitable distance there was still an awful lot of white space but now, instead of being mere nothingness, it was quite clearly the waters of two mighty rivers in collision. I have never again felt quite the same about "nothing."

Knead clay to make a pot,
but it's the nothing inside
that gives you the
use of the vessel.

From the Tao Te Ching

Must I conquer my ego?

Many religions make an issue of the need for individuals to conquer their egotistical urges. You can find this attitude fairly commonly in Zen Buddhism. I knew a teacher who made his students sweep up leaves on windy days, ostensibly because the resulting frustration was supposed to help them overcome their ego. Of course the true reason he did it was just that it's fun to boss people about. If you take Zen seriously then you know that bothering about a thing (whether to encourage or deny it) is a form of attachment. Habitually thinking, "I'm a really wonderful person!" may be an attachment to ego but thinking, "I'm really just an insignificant little worm who'd better do as my master tells me," is no better. Forget your ego! Just let it go. It's like a scratch—if you keep itching it won't get better. If you keep on with your zazen and stop worrying about rights and wrongs you will gradually begin to get it right.

Acknowledgments

I can't remember a time when I didn't know Zen stories and koans. They used be a complete mystery to me, but that was part of their attraction and I became determined to discover their secrets. I soon learned most of them by heart and it is these personal versions that I give you here. Those who want more scholarly fare can look up the official versions in any library or Zen Internet site.

My journey of discovery was made possible only by the work of some important pioneers. There are far too many to mention but some of the most influential were translators such as Paul Reps and Nyogen Senzaki. Then there were interpreters such as Christmas Humphreys, John Blofeld, and Alan W. Watts. Finally, there were teachers. In particular I am delighted to have the opportunity to express my heartfelt thanks to Shunryu Suzuki. Although he died when I was still in my teens, he left a rich legacy from which I and many others continue to benefit. No one did as much, not only to bring Zen to the West, but also to help it flourish in unfamiliar soil.

Oh, and I mustn't forget Daruma. His fearsome gaze has long been a source of inspiration for which I remain deeply grateful.